Teach Your Dog

IRISH

I think this is a GREAT idea! I LOVE it!
A charming way to help keep spoken Irish alive.

MARIAN KEYES, AUTHOR

A great way to celebrate heritage in a fun and
educational way.

ART PARKINSON, ACTOR, 'GAME OF THRONES'

Funny & surprisingly clever books. Love. Love.

DAWN FRENCH, ACTOR & COMEDIAN

Anne Cakebread not only has the best
name in the Universe, she has also come
up with a brilliantly fun book which will help
humans and canines learn new languages.

RICHARD HERRING, COMEDIAN

Teach Your Dog

IRISH

Anne Cakebread

Thank you to:
Helen, Marcie, Frieda and Lily, my family,
friends and neighbours in St Dogmaels for all
their support and encouragement, Carolyn at
Y Lolfa, and James January-McCann for Irish
translations and pronunciations.
Go raibh maith agat.

First impression 2019

© Anne Cakebread & Y Lolfa Cyf., 2019

Illustrations and design by Anne Cakebread

ISBN: 978-1-912631-09-4

Published and printed in Wales on paper from well-maintained
forests by Y Lolfa Cyf., Talybont, Ceredigion, SY24 5HE Wales
e-mail ylolfa@ylolfa.com
website www.ylolfa.com
tel +44 1970 832 304
fax +44 1970 832 782

Teach
Your Dog
Irish

"Hello"

"Dia duit"

pron:

"Djee-a ghwit"

'a'
as in
'ago'

make a
sound at
the back of
your throat
like you're
gargling

"Come here"

"Tar anseo"

pron:
"Tar un-shaw"

"Don't!"

"Ná déan!"

pron:
"Nah Jane!"

"Do you want
a cuddle?"

"Ar mhaith
leat barróg?"

pron:

"Er wah lyaat
bar-ogue?"

pronounce
this
'r'

emphasise
this
syllable

"Catch!"

"Beir air!"

pron:
"Bear**zh** air**zh**!"

'zh'
as in
'**Zh**ivago'

"Fetch!"

"Téigh ar a thóir!"

pron:

"Chay e<u>r</u> <u>a</u> hor<u>zh</u>!"

pronounce this 'r'

'a' as in '<u>a</u>go'

'zh' as in '<u>Zh</u>ivago'

"Leave it!"

"Fág é!"

pron:
"Fohg <u>ay</u>!"

'ay'
as in
's<u>ay</u>'

"Sit!"

"Suigh!"

pron:
"Sea!"

"Naughty!"

"Dána!"

pron:
"Daw-na!"

"Stay!"

"Fan!"

pron:
"Fan!"

"Bathtime"

"Am folcadáin"

pron:
"Am fol-ka-doyne"

"Bedtime"

"Am leapan"

pron:
"Am lyap-n"

"Lunchtime"

"Am lóin"

pron:
"Am loan"

"Are you full?"

"An bhfuil tú lán?"

pron:
"Un will too lawn?"

"All gone"

"Ídithe"

pron:
"Ee-deh huh"

"Good morning"

"Dia duit
ar maidin"

pron:

"Djee-a
ghwit
er mwar-jin"

'a'
as in
'ago'

make a
sound at the
back of your
throat like
you're
gargling

pronounce
this
'r'

"Goodnight"

"Oíche mhaith"

pron:

"Ee-<u>ch</u>-yuh wah"

'ch' as in 'Lo<u>ch</u> Ness'

"Don't scratch"

"Ná tochais"

pron:
"Noh to<u>ch</u>-wish"

'ch'
as in
'Lo<u>ch</u>
Ness'

"Let's go..."

"Fág seo..."

pron:
"**Fohg sho...**"

'o'
as in
'h<u>o</u>t'

"Go down"

"Síos leat"

pron:
"Sheece lyat"

"Up you go"

"Suas leat"

pron:
"Sue-uss lyat"

"Go straight ahead"

"Téigh díreach ar aghaidh"

pron:
"Chay jeer-u<u>ch</u> e<u>r</u> eye"

'ch'
as in
'Lo<u>ch</u>
Ness'

pronounce
this
'r'

"Go left"

"Téigh ar chlé"

pron:

"Chay e<u>r</u> <u>ch</u>lay"

'<u>ch</u>'
as in
'Lo<u>ch</u>
Ness'

pronounce
this
'r'

"Go right"

"**Téigh ar dheis**"

pron:

"*Chay er yesh*"

pronounce
this
'r'

"Turn left"

"Cas ar chlé"

pron:

"Cass er chlay"

'ch' as in 'Loch Ness'

pronounce this 'r'

"Turn right"

"Cas ar dheis"

pron:

"Cass er yesh"

pronounce
this
'r'

"Get down!"

"Síos leat!"

pron:
"Sheece lyat!"

"Do you
want to play?"

**"Ar mhaith
leat spraoi?"**

pron:

"E<u>r</u> wah lyat spree?"

*pronounce
this
'r'*

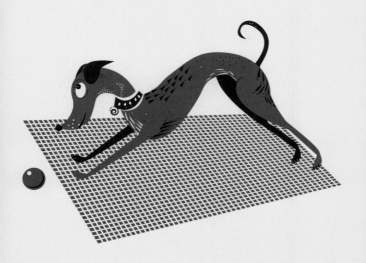

"Lie down!"

"Luigh síos!"

pron:
"Lee sheece!"

"Say 'please'!"

"Abair
'le do thoil'!"

pron:

"**A-boyzh** '*leh duh hill*'!"

'a'
as in
'm**a**n'

'zh'
as in
'**Zh**ivago'

"Can I have the ball?"

"An féidir liom an liathróid a fháil?"

pron:
"Un fate-<u>zhizh</u> lyom un lee-roweet <u>a</u> oil?"

'zh' as in '<u>Zh</u>ivago'

'a' as in '<u>a</u>go'

"Can I have a
cup of tea?"

**"An féidir liom
cupán tae
a fháil?"**

pron:
**"Un fate-<u>zhizh</u>
lyom
<u>coo</u>-pohn
tay
<u>a</u> oil?"**

'oo'
as in
'b<u>oo</u>k'

'zh'
as in
'<u>Zh</u>ivago'

'a'
as in
'<u>a</u>go'

"Very clever"

"An-chliste"

pron:

"Ahn-<u>lh</u>ish-tyuh"

put your tongue on your gums behind your teeth and blow

"It's warm"

"Tá sé te"

pron:
"Tar shay te"

'e'
as in
'm<u>e</u>t'

"It's cold"

"Tá sé fuar"

pron:
"Tar shay foo-er"

pronounce
this
'r'

"It's hot"

"Tá sé
brothallach"

pron:

"Tar shay <u>bro</u>-hol-<u>och</u>"

emphasise
this
syllable

'o'
as in
'h<u>o</u>t'

'och'
as in
'<u>Loch</u>
Ness'

"It's raining"

"Tá sé ag
cur báistí"

pron:

"Tar shay egg
c<u>oo</u>r boh-shtee"

'oo'
as in
'b<u>oo</u>k'

pronounce
this
'r'

"Are you happy?"

"An bhfuil áthas ort?"

pron:

"Un will aw-huss ort?"

pronounce
this
'r'

"Who's snoring?"

"Cé atá ag srannadh?"

pron:

"K-yay _a_tar egg s-ran-uh?"

'a' as in '_a_go'

"Have you got enough room?"

"**An bhfuil spás do dhóthain agat?**"

pron:

"Un will sporce duh g<u>ho</u>-han ug-ut?"

make a sound at the back of your throat like you're gargling

'o' as in 'g<u>o</u>'

"I won't be long"

"Ní bheidh
mé fada"

pron:
"Knee vay
may far-duh"

"Be quiet!"

"Bí ciúin!"

pron:
"Be <u>cu</u>ne!"

'cu'
as in
'<u>cu</u>be'

"Who did that?"

"Cé a rinne é sin?"

pron:

"K-yay a rin-yuh ay shin?"

'a' as in 'ago'

"There's a queue for the loo"

"Tá scuaine le haghaidh an leithris"

pron:

"Tar sk<u>oo</u>n-yuh le high un lerus"

'oo' as in 'sh<u>oo</u>t'

1

"**aon**"

pron:
"<u>ain</u>"

'ain'
as in
'r<u>ain</u>'

2

"**dó**"

pron:
"*dough*"

3

"trí"

pron:
"tree"

4

"ceathair"

pron:
"kya-high-<u>zh</u>"

'zh'
as in
'<u>Zh</u>ivago'

5

"cúig"

pron:

"c<u>oo</u>-ig"

'oo' as in 'sh<u>oo</u>t'

6

"sé"

pron:

"shay"

7

"seacht"

pron:

"shar-<u>cht</u>"

'ch'
as in
'Lo<u>ch</u>
Ness'

8

"ocht"

pron:

"<u>ocht</u>"

'och'
as in
'Lo<u>ch</u>
Ness'

9

"naoi"

pron:

"knee"

"Thank you"

"Go raibh
maith agat"

pron:
"Guh rev
mah ug-ut"

"Merry Christmas"

"Nollaig
Shona"

pron:
"Nol-ig Hon-uh"

'o'
as in
'hot'

"Congratulations!"

"Comhghairdeas!"

pron:
"Coe-g̲har-jiss!"

make a
sound at
the back
of your throat
like you're
gargling

"Happy Birthday"

"Lá breithe sona duit"

pron:

"Law bre-huh son-uh ghwit"

'o' as in 'hot'

make a sound at the back of your throat like you're gargling

"I love you"

"Tá grá agam duit"

pron:

"Tar grah ug-um ghwit"

make a sound at the back of your throat like you're gargling

"Goodbye"

"Slán"

pron:
"Slawn"

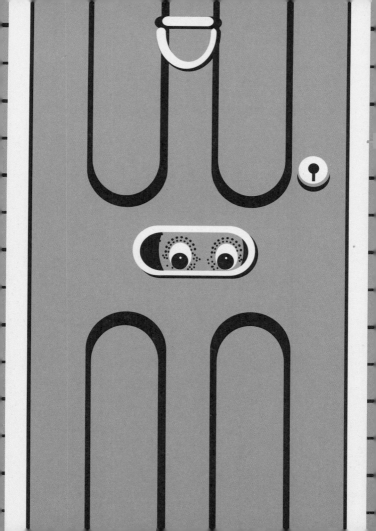

Other titles in this series include:

Teach Your Dog Welsh
Teach Your Cat Welsh
Teach Your Dog Cornish
Teach Your Dog Māori
Teach Your Dog Japanese
(Rugby World Cup 2019 Travel Edition)
Teach Your Dog Gaelic